# FIRE STICK:

2020 User Guide to Master the Potentials and Unlock The Hidden Features of Your Amazon Fire Stick with 50 Tips & Tricks. Troubleshooting Tips included.

ISBN: 9798669315603

# CONTENTS

# Introduction

The Fire Stick is a small mechanism that you can connect easily to your personal computer, and it has more significance than the universal serial bus flash. You will find the device in little boxes close to the television and include it through the HDMI cord. Just like what you call it, it is a very small and stick-like mechanism that functions easily with the computer system. It has a height of 3.4 inches and 1.2 inches in width. The device is a standard HDMI plug, and you should attach it to any available port on your television. The TV should have an HDCP suited HDMI port, and then you can attach a micro Universal Serial Bus power cord and select a Wireless network. It also comes with the Stick and a small virtual help voice remote. Users can utilize the interface of the Stick to interact with the digital help mechanism. You can use the help mechanism to unlock several skills and instructions. One entertaining advantage of the help mechanism is that you can use it to play music with a simple tap on the mic button control.

Users can access a different collection of movies and shows to watch through prime video. But before you begin, you need to input your profile information and connect with the remote. There are several important sections that you should navigate through, like the apps, shows, search, settings, and so on. The mechanism interface starts in the home section. You can utilize the track pad for navigation to go through different segments and contents, and it is on the remote. You can use the center of the track pad whenever you want to select one or multiple items instead of pressing lots of buttons. The introduction of the virtual voice help makes it easy for users to perform several tasks with the use of their voice by simply tapping the mic and pass the commands with their voice.

The manufacturing company also includes the parental control feature in the Stick to help parents control what the children watch. In the setup process, users can set passwords which the children will require before they watch or play some certain contents or even buy anything online. You can utilize the Stick without the need for the virtual voice help because you can find its application for your type of device in their various stores. You can use your voice to search for anything and also perform on-screen navigation. If you have a voice recognition mechanism, it is easy to link it with the Stick and manage the machine with different types of command.

The Stick has two different versions and

you can select whichever version you want and enjoy. It is advisable to buy the device from the manufacturing company store although you will also find them with several retailers.

# Chapter 1 – Amazon Streaming Products Fire TV vs. Fire Stick

There have been lots of options for relaxation in the past few months. You can decide to visit a cinema to see a movie or just lay on your sofa and spend the night in watching movies. But you can enhance your in-house movie experience, and mechanisms like the Stick can help you achieve that task. You will find lots of transmitting providers on the market, but Amazon provides two famous transmitting devices, which are Fire television and the Fire Stick. They function separately and differently for streaming. The manufacturing company introduced the first-generation Fire television in the year 2014, a small box that you can attach into ports to give you entry into Prime, Netflix, and other providers. The second came into existence in the year 2015, and has adequate power for processing, and blended with the digital help. After its launch, they introduced the Stick first generation, a tiny and economic streaming mechanism, and in October of the year 2014. As an alternative to the box concept, it is a tiny stick that you can link easily to different ports.

## Fire TV

It is a mechanism with various transmitting advantages and has lots of top-notch attributes as well as the power to provide a wonderful and long-lasting experience. It has a slender square structure, a quality HDMI cord, and a micro Universal Serial Bus port for the power. You will find it at the back of the television, which will save you lots of stress. The television is very easy to use, attach the Universal Serial Bus cord and adapter into a wall socket, and link to the cyberspace utilizing Wireless or an additional Adapter whenever you want to see a show or film. The virtual help can help users in locating the start and manage virtual content for transmission. You should pair the television with voice recognition mechanisms so that you can use it for hands-free control when it's time for a movie. Users can also utilize the digital help through the virtual assistant remote to play songs, get weather updates, and hear the news of everything going on around you.

## Fire Stick

It offers a similar transmission experience, just like the television. It contains several fun advantages, excellent quality of pictures, and the power to manage content with a digital assistant remote. The stick mechanism weights 1.1 ounces and has a similar shape with the Universal Serial Bus drive and not the square shape of the Fire television. Because of its lightweight, you can place it easily at the back of the HDTVs and functions ideally for non-stop fun. The Fire television Stick does not require a lot of effort to function. Plug it to the HDTV, plug the adapter, get internet with Wireless, and then the streaming of films and shows can begin. The digital help remote comes automatically with television Stick. It lets you utilize the virtual help to search for flicks and manage your playback using your voice.

# Streaming advantages

## Fire TV

The television offers a wonderful watching experience ad gives users access to over one hundred thousand shows and movies. It also provides options for users to view live television without cable.

Captivating fun: viewing a show on a standard computer or television does not give you all the influencing feels, but it has the opposing effect. It makes it a perfect option for a few top-notch television models. It also provides excellent picture quality as well as HDR for realistic images and transmission at 60 fps, which eradicate every blurry visual display. For audio enhancement, it is suitable for Dolby Digitals.

Virtual content access: It contains over one hundred thousand shows and movies from various providers. You can go through YouTube while on your sofa and utilizing the TV. However, some services come with subscription fees.

No cable: You can view live television in two ways. Utilize an HD transmitter linked to the TV for free broadcasting networks or watch episodes with payment made to DirectTV.

## Fire Stick

If you want a cost-effective transmitting multimedia mechanism that provides attributes similar to the television, the Stick is a wonderful option. It has a lot of advantages, like image and audio, and options to watch live television without cable.

- **Atmosphere:** Experiences that improves the senses is one of the best, and the television Stick will give you that and swings you into action. It functions with few top-notch television models. It offers an atmosphere higher than the standard computer, tablet.

- **Large content checklist:** Users can view virtual content from providers if they pay to transmit media sources.

- **Watch programs sans cable:** Similar to the television, and the tv Stick lets you view live television by utilizing an HD transmitter linked to the tv for broadcasting network access.

- **Active streaming:** It links with ports, and you require a Wireless connection to view your preferred films even if you are away from your home. It comes in a slim shape, and can compact stream anytime, and anywhere.

## Fire TV

Anytime you purchase the television bundle, you will find a digital help Remote inside it. It provides a seamless streaming encounter and comes with several home advantages. The device can find, open, and listen to contents easily with just a simple tap. You can give instructions like, "virtual help, search for action sci-fi," or "digital assistant, proceed to the next movie," and it will execute that command. You can also go through your preferred flicks without switching channels. Anytime you use the virtual help on the television, it provides more transmitting functions.

## Fire stick

The television Stick bundle comes with the digital help Remote for top-quality streaming. The digital help echo can help users locate, load, and manage films with voice instructions. Just pass commands like, "digital help, search for romance movies," or "virtual help, stop," while you are viewing virtual content on Netflix or others. Tap the microphone control-key if you want to ask for anything from the virtual help.

# Chapter 2 – How to Setup your Amazon Fire Stick

The Stick is the economic streaming mechanism that gives you the ability you view a lot of films and episodes through Amazon and also utilize different applications for your tasks.

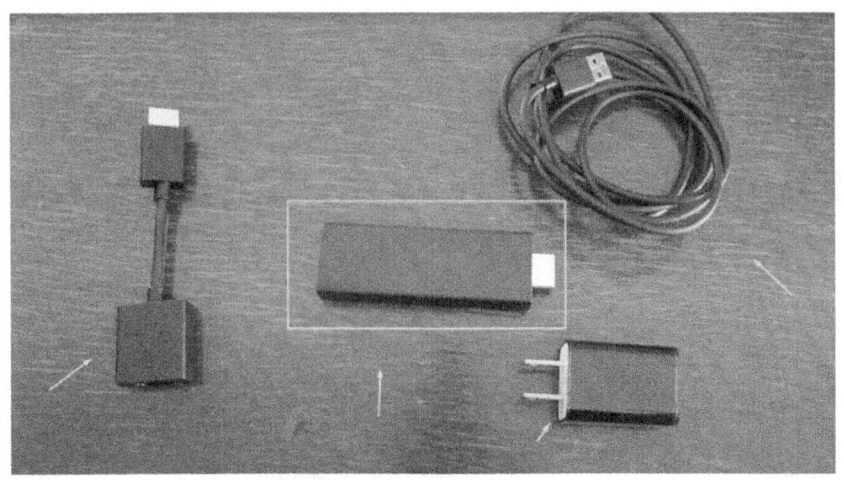

## Items inside the box

- Virtual assistant mechanism speech controller

- Adapter

- Batteries

- HDMI Extension cord

It comes with an excellent cord and is larger than the cable link port. For this reason, it may obstruct a few other ports. So, whenever you utilize the cord, it will not have any form of blocking.

## Items needed

- **10 Mbps Wireless cyberspace network:** You need an excellent cyberspace connection that has at least 8 Mbps and can transmit video of at least 1080p. You can perform some tasks without wireless because it does not have a connection port for ethernet.

- **A profile:** Anytime you buy the Stick, it will think you have a profile, but if that is not the case, you should create it. Utilize it with Prime because it comes with additional advantages like watching a complete show or films.

- **1080p visual display:** It functions properly with every visual display with HDMI ports, and also monitors. The first version of the Stick cannot support 4k, and if you want that advantage, then you should purchase a 4k mechanism.

# Setup

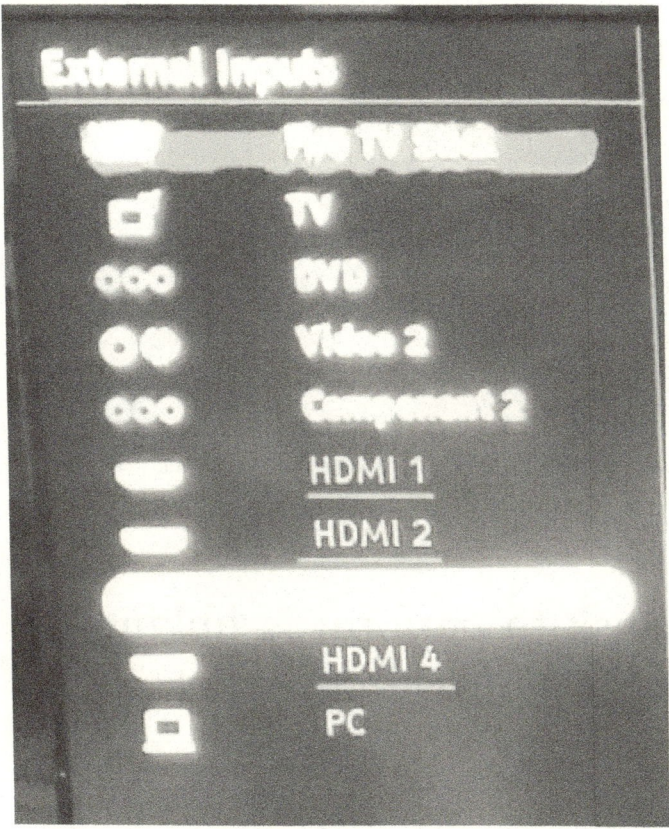

After getting all the required items, you can easily execute the setup process.

Link the Stick to the television and adapter. Toggle it on and navigate to the right HDMI port with the remote.

## Pair remote

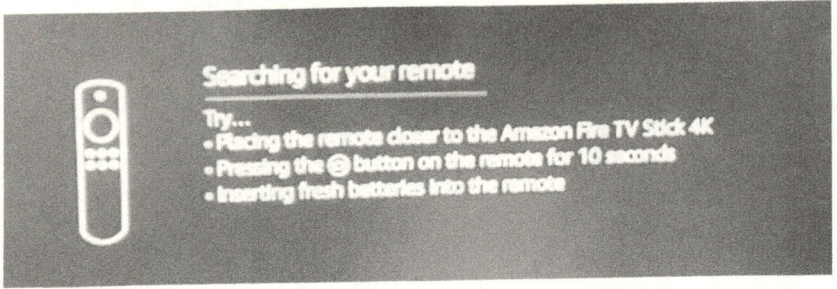

The first task to perform is linking the virtual help remote with the Stick.

Place the batteries. They are not regular ones and ensure that they face one direction.

Tap and hold the home control key on the remote for about 10 seconds until it can locate the Stick.

After pairing, tap play to proceed

Choose your desired language

Tap OK.

## Link to wifi

Highlight your desired Network and select it

Type your pass-key.

Navigate your way to a character and tap. After that, click on play.

# Register stick

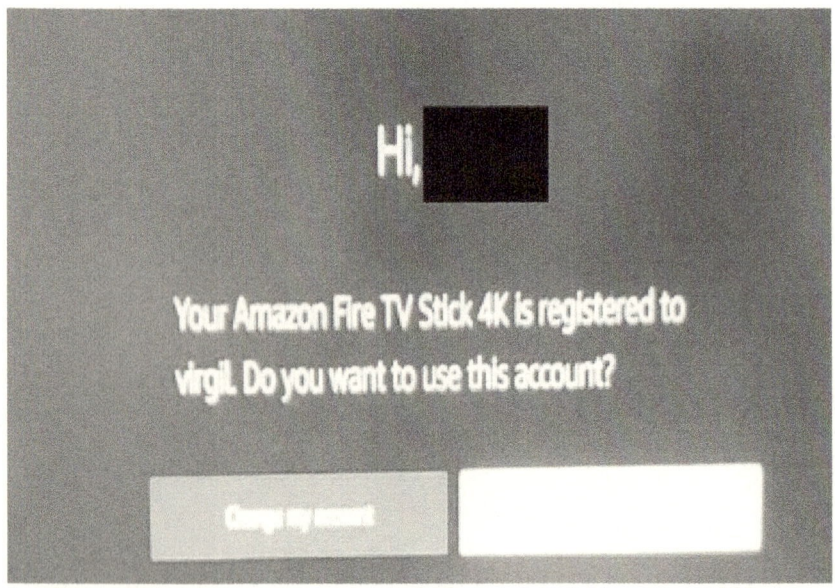

You will require your amazon profile to register the Stick.

In the process of registering the mechanism, tap select and input your email, then tap play.

Type your pass-key and tap play.

The Stick will hold a record of that profile. Then the visual confirmation display pops up, displaying the name of the account. Tap select to move forward.

## Store Wireless Passwords

You can store Wireless pass-key on the television stick to the Amazon cloud. With this done, all the manufacturing company mechanisms with the account links immediately to the Network. You should also know that it is not advisable to store pass-keys on the internet.

Password security lets users add parental controls. Parents can set pass-keys for the mechanism that the kids will need whenever they want to watch things online.

Users can also ignore the controls for parents and continue, but it will give the kids free access to do whatever they want.

But if you want to utilize it, turn the feature on, and it will demand a pin.

Input the pin and tap allow

Tap OK.

## The Intro Video

The next visual display will play a video, teaching how to utilize the virtual help voice instructions with the Stick.

# Manage and track Data usage

The next visual display gives you the ability to manage and track the amount of data the Stick utilizes. It is particularly helpful if you are on a budget.

Tap set up later if you do not want to know the amount of data the Stick consumes.

Tap allows data tracking to set limits on data.

In the next pop-up visual display, choose the quality you want.

Set the amount of data you want to utilize

Now you can see the visual display

update when it reaches the limit set.

## Navigate through stick menu

It can be hard at first, but it is very easy to utilize and understand. It can take some time to learn and get accustomed to it, and it becomes fun. What you should know is that any logo with a yellow is the point of the cursor. When you choose to play, it performs the task on the marked item.

Scroll and select any item of your choice.

## Obtain a film or episode's Menu

Whenever you get to a movie visual display, every Data you require is right there. You can see the show's length when they produced it, and lots more. There are options like:

View with Prime

View Trailer

Include the item to Watch list

Collections and films

You should know that it's not every movie trailer that you can access the television Stick. Any show you included in a watch list will display in your watch list within the Home visual display.

For television episodes, when you choose to watch now on Prime, it begins the first chapter of the beginning season.

Feel free to choose a specific chapter by proceeding to shows, where you can access all of them.

Tap Down inside a movie page to locate related things list.

## Utilize X-Ray on the television Stick

The virtual help Remote and X-Ray merge to provide things with Prime Video. Because the manufacturing company owns IMDb, you can obtain data about that scene you happen to be viewing.

Tap Up to authorize necessary X-Ray, when the video is still in progress. It displays the participants in that scene. Tap Up once more to halt the video and produce the entire Menu.

# Chapter 3 – Tips for your Fire Stick

## Enjoy movies

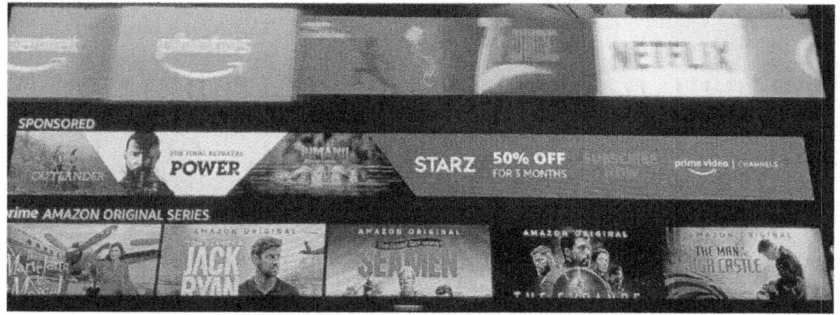

To watch a movie at night without disturbing anybody in the house with you, you should utilize the headphones. Even the loudest episodes will output equal loud fun if you utilize the headphones. The unique category for movie nights is "comedy." To link the headphones, proceed to settings, then controllers and devices. Now you can choose the gadget that you want to link with headphones.

## Preventing Targeted commercials

You can have customized commercials sent to users, depending on their choices. You can utilize the turn-off feature. This feature will stop any targeted commercials from displaying on the television. You will still get adverts, but they will be standard and do not depend on random clicks. To stop targeted commercials, proceed to settings, then select preferences and then commercial ID.

# Choosing                    customized Screensavers With images

To modify the images with another one that you took or your preferred one as your screensaver, proceed to display settings. To achieve this, you need to utilize prime images. It stores the large cloud of images that consist of a prime bundle.

## Modify Name

Anytime you purchase a mechanism from Amazon such as the tv sticks, it comes with a name from the manufacturing company. If you have similar mechanisms, it can create confusion, particularly when you buy applications and want them to reach the appropriate mechanism. Navigate to control contents and system page and choose the system tab. Select your mechanism and choose the Edit link.

## Eliminate speech Records

However, the manufacturing company keeps a record of all the tasks you perform from the voice search to the Fire television. It enhances perfection, but you can delete any of your recordings. Find your way to the control Content and gadget page, select your mechanism, and choose to eradicate speech Recordings, choose then eradicate.

# Remove speech search

Users have the freedom to remove speech searches one after the other via the virtual assistant phone app, proceed to Settings >then select History, tap an entry for anything you said, and select Delete.

# Remove Data

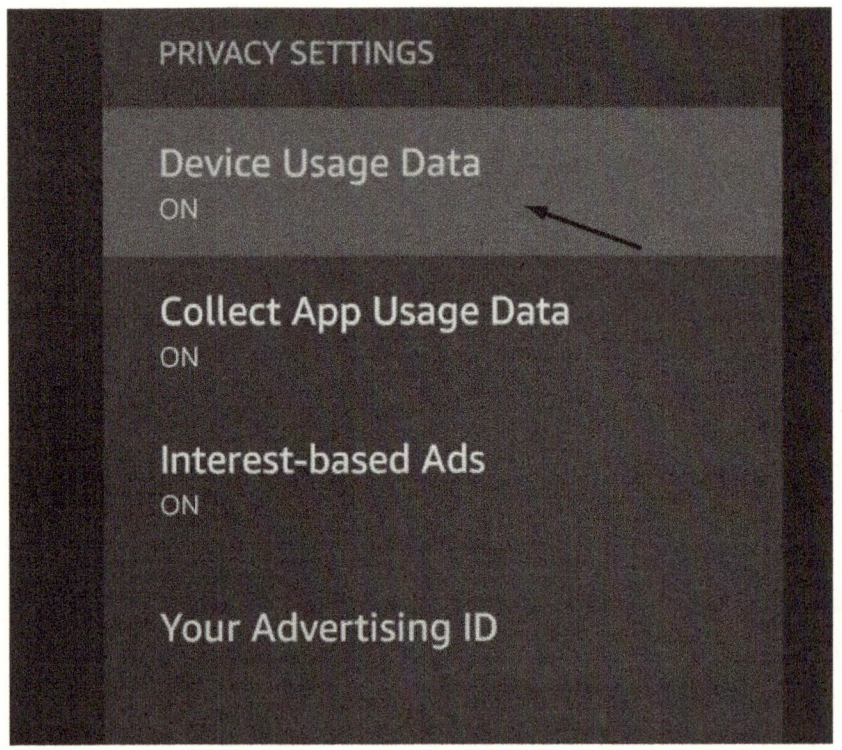

To remove data whenever you want to, launch the television interface and go to Settings > then Apps > controlled Installed Apps. Choose apps like

Amazon songs and pick remove Data, you can also free Cache to restart.

## Stop commercials

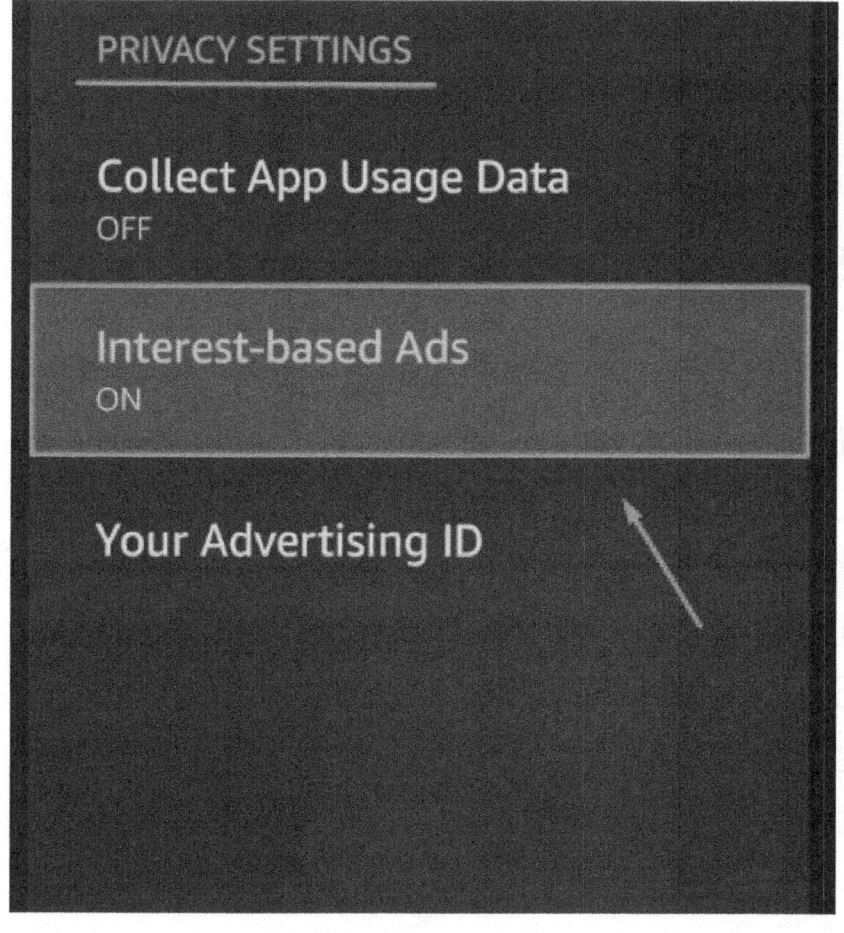

Although you cannot stop the television from doing commercials, you can halt it from tracing you. Switch off tracing by navigating to Settings > then Preferences, privacy, and change cyberspace-Based Adverts to off.

## Stop Appstore from storing Data

Users can turn off the store's ability to collate data on the rate at which it happens over a specific period of utilization of downloaded applications. To perform that task, proceed to settings, select preferences, privacy, and toggle the option off.

# Speak to the television

You can access your voice searches through the virtual help application Because of the television functions perfectly with the virtual voice help. You can manage the television with a close-by voice recognition mechanism. Just pass instructions like "digital help, play the song I will love you forever.

## Fire television Remote Application

The first television Stick does not have a speech search alternative. Fix that by obtaining the television remote application. The mobile should be on one Wireless Network with the television to function properly.

Whenever you first launch the application, the name should display on the mobile visual display, select it, then input your four-digit pin, and it will give you total control.

## Disallow Auto-Play Video

On the television interface, proceed to Settings > then choose Preferences > featured proportions and switch off the enable Auto play. In the process of performing that task, you should also switch off enable Audio Auto play.

## Survey what you are viewing

Anytime you are viewing a video on

Amazon, you can easily obtain information by utilizing the X-Ray attribute. Press up or the down key to go through information of the cast, Locate the song playing an in which scene, and obtain trivia, and at the same time, you do not stop watching.

## Play music With Bluetooth Headphones

If you do not want to wake the neighbor or the entire household up with your late-night movies, pick up a pair of headphones and sync the device to the television. Proceed to Settings > then management and Bluetooth gadgets > Bluetooth systems. Then the audio moves to the headphones.

# Play music with cord Headphones

You can also watch movies on your device and keep the sound out of everyone's ears by utilizing headphones with universal serial bus access and then sync the device to the TV. In the process of watching the movie, just insert the card into the system, and it will play the audio in it.

## Watch Local Content

The best alternative is Plex. Acquire the multimedia server element of Plex onto a Personal Computer that has Windows or other major providers. Connect your videos, images, and audio document and launch the application on the television.

# Parent management Settings

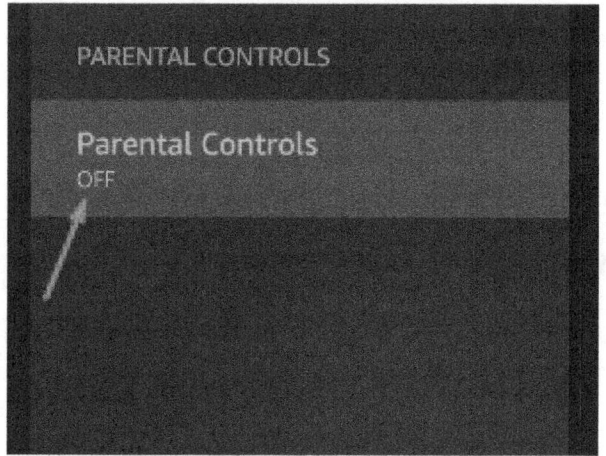

To execute that task, Proceed to Settings > then to Preference > and the Parent management, and turn it off or on. You need to input your PIN to access more important and educative content or buy on a later date.

# Mouse toggle

The television Stick remote allow you toggle in about four different sides, but you attach Chrome on it, which will enable you to utilize the cyberspace network? But because it is an Android mechanism, therefore installing it will not be difficult. To fix this issue, you can utilize an app named Mouse Toggle for the television that allows you to change the type to accurate navigation by attaching a pointer. You should acquire the application and install it, then press the play control key twice, and a dot will appear that you can utilize as a mouse toggle.

## Utilizing digital help mechanism for the television

The digital help can perform a lot of tasks when you give instructions. You can as well watch Netflix movies and other kinds of stuff if you pay its monthly payment. If you do not know how to obtain digital help on television, what you have to do is to go to settings and then select virtual help and enjoy the company of your new personal help.

# Forget the Remote

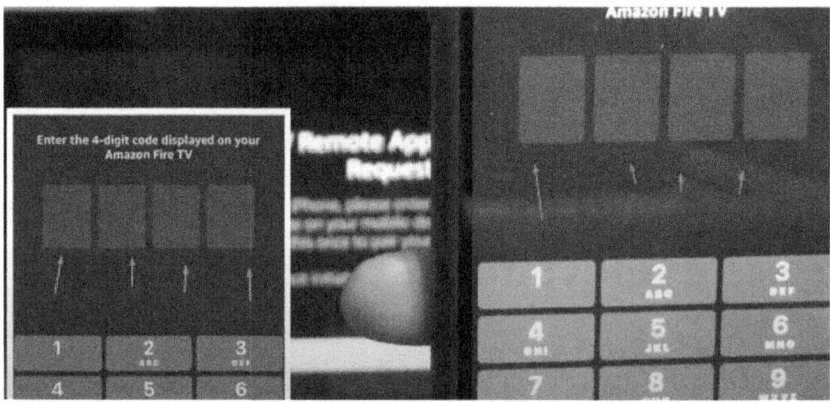

If you want to utilize the mechanism when you are not with the remote, there is an application that will assist you with the android and iOS problems. You can merge the virtual assistant instructions into it. You can navigate through the applications and its simple interface with the same pattern. It also lets you utilize the keyboard to enter pass-keys easily.

# Connect to the Hotel Wireless

The issue here is that the hotel Wireless needs a web browser to sign in. The Stick permits this. Therefore, proceed to Settings > then Network and search for Network you wish to attach to and select it. If it requires a login page, it will indicate it. To move in-between fields, select the menu control-key (). It is good to utilize the intelligent mobile-based remote if you want to fill in fields. Whenever you link the television Stick, the browser will close.

## Repair Remote control

If the current remote does not link to the

television or its Stick, it is a straightforward problem to solve. Press and hold the home control key for a few seconds. That often solves the problem.

## Reload with Remote

Tap and hold the Play control-key and choose the button at the same time for four seconds. Then you will get a color splash and logo telling you that the television is rebooting.

## Utilize Bluetooth headset

Playing the television audio can sometimes be complex. However, there are lots of alternatives. Intelligent gadgets like the television Stick let you utilize your preferred headsets and speakers. Proceed to Settings > then to managers & Bluetooth mechanisms > select Other Bluetooth mechanisms and choose the mechanism that you wish to link. And you can enjoy it.

## Watch Live

If you pay a subscription to Prime stations such as HBO and so on, then you can go through everything. You should also know that there is content for you if you do not pay for live television, such as Pluto TV and so on.

# Utilize mouse toggle for specific apps

Some applications have the touch device attribute that you can utilize on your smartphone. You can sideload the apps on the Stick, although it can be difficult to find your way through such apps. You should get the mouse toggle app for the remote navigation because it has a pointer for the mechanism.

## Set TV display to fit videos

It is an effortless task to perform on the Stick, to perform it, launch Settings on the mechanism.

Select sounds and display

Tap display and calibrate it

Tap the up and down control key to modify its look

## Reset apps

Anytime you perform that task on an application, it goes back to its original settings. Perform the task with the following steps:

Launch Settings and tap apps

Tap control installed apps

Select the faulty app and tap clear Cache if that is your purpose.

Select clear Data is that is what you want and tap clear again.

## Get an IPTV Subscription

You will get some high-quality IPTV services when you gain access to thousands of satellite channels on a paid sub. They provide affordable solutions when you compare them to other providers.

## Allow apps from unknown sources

Perform the task with the following steps:

Launch Settings and tap my fire television

Launch the developer options and modify the settings

Ensure that the apps from unknown

sources are on

## Modify app store settings

Perform the task with the following steps:

Launch Settings and tap the option apps

Launch the app store and modify its settings.

## Automatic Updates:

Ensure that it status on to enable apps to update regularly. The attribute work with apps obtained from the manufacturing company and not the other sources to avoid side loads.

## Additional links to the market:

Some apps come with different links that redirect back to the manufacturing company store before you can install them. Tap the option and select ask before you open.

## In-App Purchases:

Ensure that the option stays off. It prevents unnecessary and accidental purchases, especially with kids.

# Notifications:

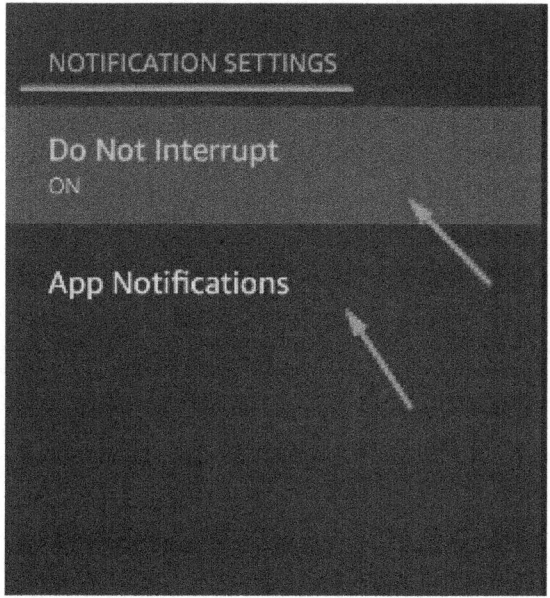

If you do not want the alerts to disturb you, you can simply turn the feature off, but if you want to receive regular alerts about your activities, you should leave it on.

## Keep cloud apps:

You should also keep this option off if you want to see the apps list that you have but yet to install. The mechanism saves the app in the cloud so that it does not take up much space on the device.

## Modify display settings

If you want to modify your display settings, the below steps will help you:

Launch Settings and tap sounds and display.

Tap display, and you can modify

# Video resolution:

Select the resolution you want. Although, it is advisable to utilize auto mode so the mechanism can decide which resolution is best for you.

# Color depth:

You should select between eight, ten, or twelve bits.

# Color format:

Ensure that you set auto and let the mechanism select the right format that you can utilize.

## Free Night for films

You are familiar with going to the IMDb to view what you are seeing, but think about utilizing it to view something? The television has several shows and episodes.

## Get Home quicker

Going through HDMI choices to reach the television can be crazy sometimes. Click Menu and find CEC and choose it. Now on the television, proceed to Settings > then Sounds and examine the mechanism Control is on. When you do that, tapping the Home control-key on the remote will bring rights to the TV.

# YouTube for Fire television

Although that service is unavailable on the television stick, you can use it on Android. Therefore we can work around it. The Stick consists of the application logo, and you are free to tap it, now you need to acquire Silk or keep on utilizing Firefox. Get any of these apps, and enjoy the privilege. Now anytime you choose the logo, it takes you to the service interface, and you can enjoy your videos.

## Utilize Universal Serial Bus OTG and transform the Stick to television

The Stick contains an OTG functionality.

You can utilize the function through its designed hardware and with the television. It consists of a male Micro Universal Serial Bus jack at an end, one female Universal Serial Bus at another end, and another Universal Serial Bus A Type too. You only need to link the male end to the television stick and connect the power cord to the female micro Universal Serial Bus jack that will function as a power provider. When you set everything up, you can attach a Universal Serial Bus thumb drive to the A-Type port or enhance the proportions and then attach a thumb drive. The drive will appear in your explorer.

## Put the mechanism to sleep

One amazing attribute of television stick

is that you can tap and hold the Home control key for five seconds when you are on the home visual display and have easy entry to settings and utilize the Sleep control to put the machine to sleep.

## Screen Mirroring

You can tap and hold the Home control key and then select the mirroring alternative to enter the mirror section of the television stick. Utilize this alternative on Android to find for television and then connect. And it is done.

# Utilize mobile as a keyboard

Obtain the television Remote application from your device Store and log into with one profile with the Stick. You require two intelligent phones to perform that task. One mobile will function as a remote, and the other will replicate your Wireless connection, and it's pass-key.

# Organize Apps

Every application you acquire on the television stick are all within the name apps and games. If you utilize lots of applications, you are going to enjoy this mechanism. What you have to do is to choose the application you wish to move and tap the menu control key and select Move. Then you can arrange the app anyhow you want.

## Utilize Aptoide television

The television has a collection of applications. What you should know is that television does have any illegitimate movie transmitting applications. When you launch the television, it is a normal application store that has apps with several collections, and you can get them as you please. You should know that the store can update apps that you already have automatically.

# Chapter 4 – Outstanding Capabilities of Firestick

Lots of people utilize the mechanism

because it gives them access to several television channels. Although you can achieve more with the mechanism and below are few outstanding capabilities of the Stick.

## Watch television

The mechanism lets users view different channels that they cannot find somewhere else. You can also connect the device to any television with a universal serial bus port.

## Utilize virtual help mechanism

It let users utilize the virtual help mechanism, and they can ask any type of question and utilize it the same way they use the voice recognition mechanism. If you have a paid sub to Amazon songs, you can get the virtual help mechanism to play you any type of music you want. You can also use the feature to search for any item online.

## Utilize voice search

Users can now find any type of content easily with the Stick through the voice search attribute. It can save users lots of time and help them find things quickly. The search can begin with the sound of your voice passing instructions.

# Go on holiday with the mechanism

The can function anywhere as long as there is wireless, and it is an item that you can make traveling with you to any location. It is also an important tool to take on a journey for entertainment for the kids.

## Set location

If you are the type that utilizes the virtual help mechanism for weather and local news information, it is important to set your location accurately. You can also utilize the feature for directions from one location to another.

# Toggle off Autoplay

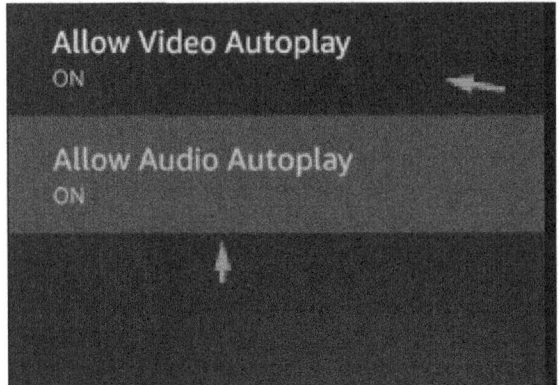

Advertisement will stay showing immediately you look through items by default, and it can be a distraction for lots of people. You can turn off the attribute that will enable you to see the show lost but without displaying its trailer.

# Utilize image as a screensaver

Users can now attach their images to the mechanism and utilize it as a screensaver. Users can decide the number of images they want to have on, and they can include several images to create a slide show. The slide show option allows several methods of customizing, and you can tweak it whichever way you want as well as determine what each pic represents.

# Eradicate apps

You will find the mechanism with preloaded apps, and lots of the apps can be useful, but you can easily eradicate the unwanted ones. Remove unwanted apps to create room for new ones.

# Chapter 5 – Best Amazon Fire Stick Apps

The Stick is a wonderful mechanism, and users can set it up easily on the television. They can now view your desired video with much comfort. Below are a few applications that function best with the Stick.

# Cinema APK

It is a top-rated Android application for films and episodes. The application consists of a vibrant group of programmers that update it regularly. It is an accumulator that gets transmission links from lots of servers in different positions.

## CatMouse

It is a beautiful application for the required content, which includes films and episodes. The app contains a lot of content you can browse and see. As also top-notch streams from the major providers on the internet. There are lots of complete-HD streams for the contents.

# CyberFlix TV

The application has a good group of films and episodes. The app obtains the transmission from different providers that you can find in the Terrarium television. You can log in with a Debrid profile to utilize the premium benefits, compete HD transmission.

# Titanium TV

This application consists of extensive collections of films and episodes and allows you to transmit them into top-notch and quality. The app obtains a few excellent links, which include a lot of complete HD transmission. You can as well log into the Debrid account and improve the number of total HD links.

## UnlockMyTV

The multimedia collection is sturdy and always reconditioned with the latest content. This application is very famous as a Cinema carbon copy.

## Stremio

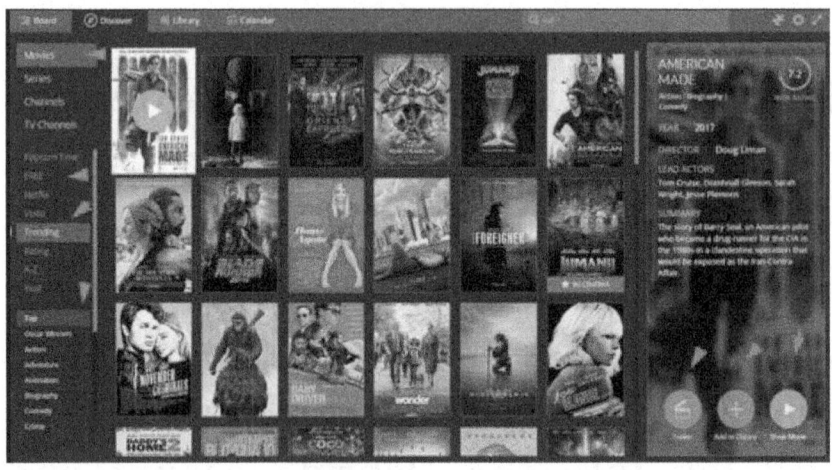

It is a cyberspace multimedia service and also aids a large number of mechanisms. The application add-ons install automatically online. It means that anytime you obtain an add-on on a tool, you can access it from every mechanism: Stremio aids official and general add-ons. With just one click, you can attach add-ons.

## Plex

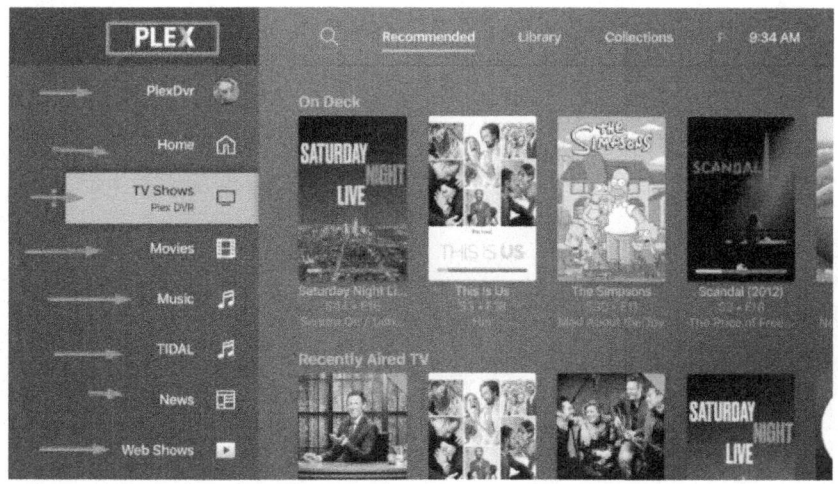

It turns your device into a multimedia hub by changing to a server and gives you entry into local and cyberspace multimedia from customer applications for an extensive collection of mechanisms, which includes the Fire stick. You can play any film or song for your computer without wires on the tool. You can acquire server plugins and get entry to boundless cyberspace multimedia on Fire stick.

## Netflix

Although it comes with a subscription, yet it remains an excellent application for Stick. It always has the latest content and very entertaining, which you will never tire you out. When you pay the subscription on the Stick, feel free to utilize one profile on lots of mechanisms.

# Morph television

Although there is a famous television called Morpheus, it is not functioning, its carbon copy the Morph television is quickly obtaining an excellent status among transmitters. The tv has the backing of a functioning group of programmers. The television updates are well-organized, and you can condition the multimedia items with the latest films and episodes.

## BeeTV

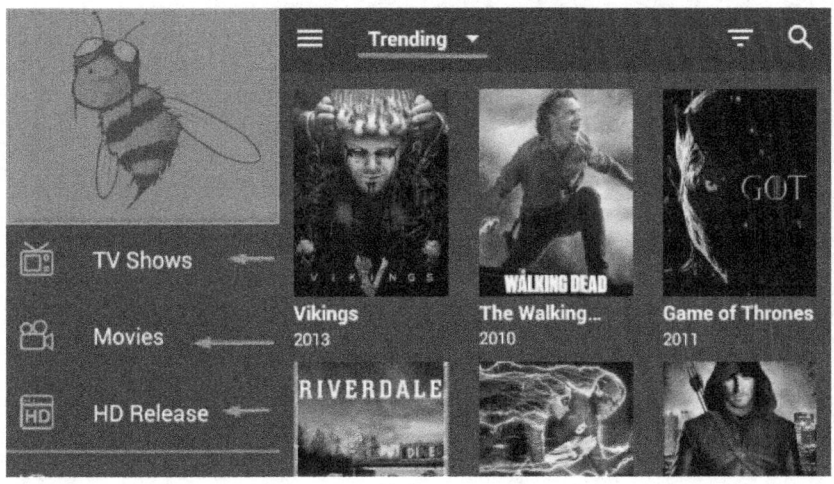

The application contains an extensive content collection that you can view for hours. The app does not organize its content. It pulls the transmission links from lots of providers online. The application contains a Debrid sign that allows the app to get top-notch links.

## TVZion

It has an attribute called one-click play; it selects the best transmitting link and immediately begins the playback. Very easy for individuals finding direct transmission, and it is well suited for the Stick remote.

## TeaTV

The application has gotten a lot of momentum since the Terrarium television went down. It has a vast collection of films and episodes and an easy interface. A large number of users prefer this application when it comes to viewing shows.

## Crackle

It is easy to locate the latest and film thrillers with less effort. Although, you require a profile on the app to give you access to its contents. If you have kids, then you will want to keep the device away from them so they do not go through adult content, something they should avoid at all costs.

## MediaBox HD

The scrapers ensure that the playback is smooth and fast. Its collection of contents updates very often and integrate new ones with satisfying streaming quality. You can also link this application with the real debris to get lots of 4k and 1080p streams.

# Typhoon TV

You can watch lots of movies for longer hours without exhaustion. It is effortless to navigate through films and videos, and it is light in weight and consists of lots of attributes. The application function properly on all gadgets.

## Redbox TV

It has a large group of channels that you can stream video smoothly. It has no bugs and light in the weight app. It also supports ads, but not the annoying ones, it is easy to navigate through the ads and close it by tapping the black control key, and it will return to the transmitting business.

## TVTap

The application offers lots of live channels from the United States and other nations. It has a simple layout, speedy, and ensures easy navigation. It also has lots of professionals behind it for updates regularly.

## Downloader

The production company store has lots of fantastic applications, and you can also get from sources outside. The Stick does not let the user obtain third-party applications via the browsers, and this is where you will utilize the downloader. You can get APK files easily from the web and install them with the downloader.

## Aptoide

It is important to add the aptoide to your collection of applications for the Stick. It has an extensive collection of different applications for the Stick. If you are searching for transmitting apps, there are lots of it in the aptoide.

## BBC iPlayer

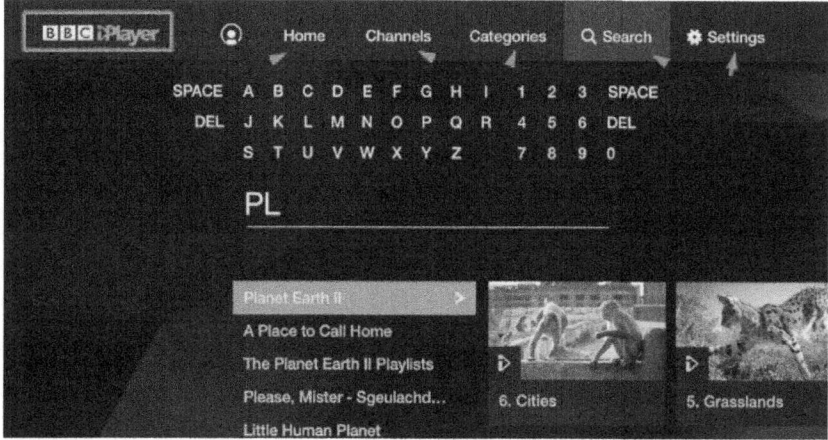

It allows users to stream virtually every content on BBC. It offers contents out of the premises of the UK via different transmitting partners.

## Pluto TV

It always has a new item for you every time. It is free to obtain, and you can begin enjoying several contents immediately after obtaining the app.

## Crunchyroll

Users will find more than twenty-five thousand series of anime on the application and can keep users entertained for a long time. The series comes in Japanese, but the app can solve the barrier because you can change the language easily.

## OneBox HD

It is a perfect free app for maximum enjoyment. The first model is not compatible with the Stick, but the most recent version functions properly with the stick mechanism.

## Mobdro

You can only obtain the app from its website. After launching the app on your television, it starts finding free videos across the world for you and direct it to your computer.

# OLA TV

It gives access to various channels from different countries. Select your desired category and tap on which channel you wish to watch.

## Live NetTV

It is the perfect app for individuals that watch live TV. You will find different categories of streaming possibilities. It also comes with a different section for shows and films.

## Sportz TV IPTV

You can begin with $14.95 a month, and

you will get over eight thousand live channels. You will find different categories of content on the app.

## Players Klub IPTV

It comes at a cost-effective price of about $8 a month. It also comes with lots of shows and films for your entertainment experience. It is reliable and offers top-quality playback for videos.

## HD Streamz

It consists of several channels. It has a radio tab for users to enjoy, but you hardly find content in them because it's a live transmission app.

## ESPN for the television

It enables sports to live transmission as well as various sporting events, and you access them all on the television. Select your desired event or sports action to watch and buy the required pass for the game.

## Sky News

It is one of the most famous twenty-four channels for new updates, and it provides access to information about different types of events and shows going on across the world.

## BBC News

It offers accurate news and one of the best outlets for the latest news and stories about events happening in the world. You can obtain the application on its official website as well as the manufacturing company store.

## YouTube

It is one of the best apps to utilize on the Stick, and you can get it from the manufacturing company store. Listening to your desired music on the right channel or searching for newly included items, you can perform all of that task on the app. You can also develop your playlist and listen to them at a convenient time.

# Twitch

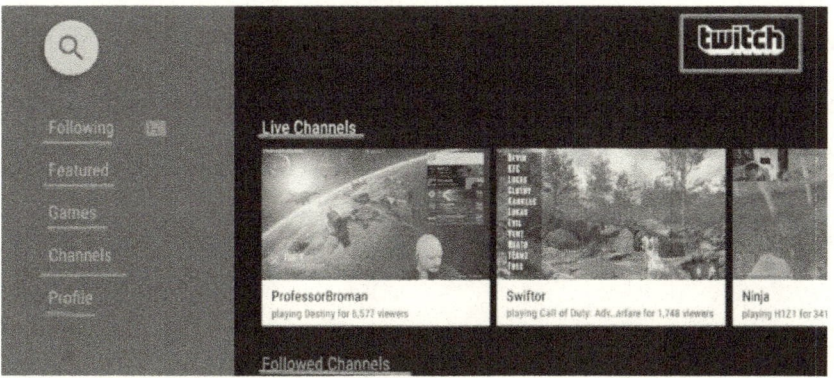

Users can find lots of live transmission for video games, and if you take an interest in a certain transmission, you can get rewards for your desired transmission and get recognized due to the number of views you get as well as your subscribers.

## Spotify

It is an app that users can utilize to play songs on various gadgets utilizing one wireless Network. You can select your song from the playlist to create the perfect mood and maximize the experience.

## Downloader

It is a wonderful utility app and a must-have on your stick mechanism. It does not matter if you want to save the desired video or sideload an app; you are going to need the service of the downloader. It is very fast and avoids time-wasting.

# FileLinked

Users can utilize this app to distribute images of songs, and so on, which makes it useful on the stick mechanism. The app also makes the process fast and efficient. You only require the code for the file from the unloader and input it into the app, and it will complete the task.

# Browser

You should proceed to the official website to get it on your gadget. You need to utilize the browser to access the website.

## Cinema HD

It is a famous app and can play the first video that functions properly with your device. It also provides a quality connection for the item you decide to watch anytime you select it.

## BeeTV APK

It provides access to essential and valid transmitting providers, which are all in the capability of your systems hardware and one that your cyberspace connection can control.

# Exodus Live television

It offers constant channel streams and does not contain lots of films and recordings. You will not find any old content on the app, but you will find the regional ones, which include Canada and the likes.

# FreeFlix HQ

It is part of the jailbreak gadgets and offers televisions shows and free flix. You will also find the app listed in an upcoming broadcast. There are several sections to find different types of streams that you want to watch, which includes wrestling and so on.

## Popcorn time

It has a straightforward interface and offers excellent media quality. You will find lots of amazing content in its library on the internet and provides content for a lifetime. You should know that this is not a website but a free app for everyone to use.

## Appflix

It provides an excellent appearance and comes with a clean layout as well as an easy to understand navigation. Users can get to watch their desired shows without any interruptions.

## Sony crackle

You can get this app from the manufacturing company store in two different channel sections. You will find the app for any type of device in the store. It is a free app that offers lots of entertainment experience.

## Euronews

It provides quick access to several new programs, including the ones that come in another language. Users can utilize foreign languages, or they can also change any type of language to English on the app.

# Firefox

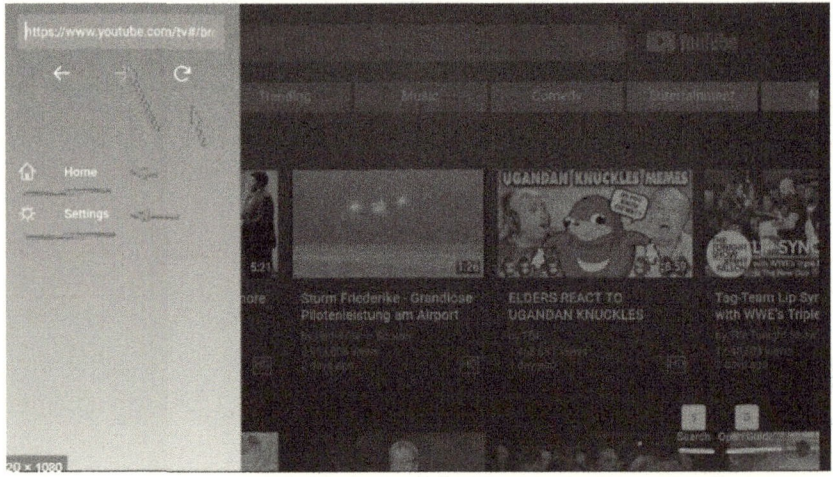

It is an open-source browser that lots of gadgets and smartphones use. It provides access to your desired sites with the utilization of the Stick.

# Chapter 6 – Troubleshooting Tips

Every user has gone through different types of problems with the stick mechanism, but have you tried fixing any of the encountered problems on your own? Below are few troubleshooting tips to help fix problems on the Stick:

## Troubleshoot Stick No Signal

Firstly, examine if the HDMI port functions correctly by linking a separate mechanism or link the Stick to a different HDMI port on the television.

Ensure that the HDMI cord is in perfect condition with no bruises. If it has any cuts, then you should replace it

Examine your cyberspace network, ensure it is active. If not, fix that issue.

## How to solve a Blank Screen problem on the Stick

Detach the power cord of your Firestick from its back and plug it back.

Disconnect the HDMI cord that links the Stick to the television and attach it back in few seconds.

Examine the cords to see if you plug them into the power provider correctly.

Tap the source control key on the

television remote and ensure the tv input is equal to the name of the port where you linked the Stick.

Set the Stick back to Factory settings.

If the television remains blank after following these steps, you should replace the HDMI cord. If that problem continues, you should purchase a new stick.

## How to solve Wireless Connection problems on the television Stick

Utilize these steps to re-link the tv to the cyberspace network.

Ensure that the cyberspace network connection is function correctly.

See if the Wireless Network chosen on the television is the correct one.

Reload the Stick.

Turn off the modem and switch it back ON after some minutes.

## Crash app issues

Users can remove any app from their device and get a new one from the store if they so desire. To achieve that task, proceed to Settings->then controlled Installed Apps and chose the application that crashes very often. Tap Force Stop-> and you can now remove Data.

## How to solve the television Stick transmission issues

Link the Stick to a wall socket power

provider rather than linking your gadget to the television's Universal Serial Bus port or another port.

If there are problems with the cyberspace network, then it will hamper transmission on the mechanism. To prevent that, ensure you select an ISP that produces an excellent cyberspace connection.

## Restart the Stick

Tap the play and select control key at once and old it for five seconds

It will reload the mechanism.

Or, proceed to settings and tap devices and restart.

# Reboot router

Switch the router off and plug it in ten seconds. It will place your Network on the fast track and solve the problem.

## Install CW

Launch Settings, select the app, and click control install apps.

Search for CW and uninstall if that is what you want.

To install it, proceed to apps and install them.

## Stick freezing issues

Disconnect the mechanism from power, return it a few seconds later and restart.

Also, proceed to settings, tap gadget options, and select restart.

## Can't remember the password for parental controls

It is a straightforward task to perform. You only need to type in the wrong pass-key into the same field more than five times, and the mechanism will make you reset it.

## Audio issues

Check if you did not mute the audio and toggle on the AV receiver.

Navigate to Settings and tap display and sounds

Turn off Dolby digitals.

## Bluetooth

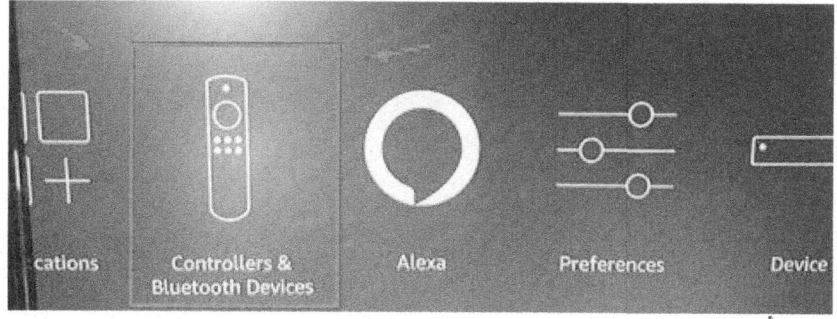

To link a Bluetooth mechanism: Give commands like "digital help, Bluetooth"

or "virtual help, pair."

If you want to link with a Bluetooth mechanism: Pass instructions like "virtual help, link with my mobile."

To detach from a Bluetooth gadget: give commands like "digital help, detach from my mobile."

Accounts and user profile

If you want to change accounts: Pass instructions like "virtual help, change profiles."


## How to solve Buffering problems on the tv Stick


Eradicate every unused application on the Stick.

Remove the video app cache on the Stick

by proceeding to Settings-> then control Installed Apps. Then, choose your preferred video application, and select Force Stop-> and then eradicate Data.

Turn off Data tracking on the Stick, and it will enhance your buffering process. To achieve this, proceed to Settings->then Preferences-> now to Data tracking and switch it off.

Switch off updates for apps you do not want. Proceed to Settings->then to Preferences-> and now update Settings and switch off the updates for individual applications.

## Troubleshoot data tracking

To achieve this, proceed to Settings->then Preferences-> now to Data tracking.

You can decide to witch the toggle on or off depending on what you want.

## How to solve Fire TV Stick Remote Issues

Examine the battery to see if you insert it correctly.

Change the batteries to new ones. Ensure that the batteries are fresh.

See if the Remote links with the Stick.

The television stick utilizes Bluetooth connection, and you should keep the remote in a range of 30 feet if you want it to function correctly.

## How to solve Application Crashes on the Fire television

Remove the application from your machine and install the app again from the manufacturing company application store.

Proceed to Settings->then controlled Installed Apps and chose the application that crashes very often. Tap Force Stop-> and you can now remove Data.

If the problem is still unsolved, you should call on the support of the app developer.

## Application update issues

Users can decide to tweak the settings for apps update on the Stick. You can decide to turn it on or leave it off. To achieve that task, Proceed to Settings->then to Preferences-> and now update Settings and switch off the updates for individual applications.

## Attach the Stick to your television HDMI port.

Turn on the television and the Stick.

Anytime the stick boots, tap the home control key for about ten seconds.

The stick pairs and it will begin to

function.

Feel free to link the Stick to about seven gadgets via Bluetooth, if you have exhausted the options, you should remove one gadget. Do that with the following steps:

Tap settings, launch Bluetooth gadgets, and controllers.

It will display the collection of connected gadgets. Select the gadget to un-pair and follow the prompt.

## The fire stick buttons not functioning

The control keys will not function well if you don't pair the Stick with the remote. Tap and hold the home control keys for about ten seconds, and it will pair again.

If the problem persists, use the following methods to repair the Stick:

## Cache issues on the Stick

Users can face different types of issues with the Stick when it comes to spaces and Cache for video apps. You can eradicate the Cache by proceeding to Settings-> then control Installed Apps. Then, choose your preferred video application, and select Force Stop-> and then eradicate Data.

## Remove the firestick plug from the power

Now hold the back, Menu and the navigation ring left part together for about twenty seconds

Take the batteries out of the remote

Turn on the Stick and wait for your home visual display

Put on the battery and wait for one to two minutes

And you are done.

## Check the stick remote compatibility

The Stick supports several intermediary controls and can serve as remotes to communicate with the gadget. Purchase remote that is compatible with your gadget.

# Check for damages on the stick remote

If the remote has damages on it, then it is time to purchase a new one, and they come at an affordable price. You will find some remotes with more control keys for some streaming applications and some with control keys for volume.

## How to Reload the Fire television Stick

Tap the Select and Play control key at once

Hold the control keys for few seconds to reload the tool.

You can also perform the same task manually, feel free to proceed to

Settings-> then system->Reload on the television utilizing the remote

## Fire Stick has no signal or streaming problems:

If your television goes off whenever you stream with the fire stick and it displays no signal on your screen, the below methods will help you fix that problem without wasting your time:

## Ensure that you have a static power light signal:

If the light signal continues to fluctuate or immediately goes off when you stream, then you have a faulty power cord, socket, or plug.

## Ensure that your socket, plug or cord is not faulty:

You should check the plug, socket, or cord very carefully. Feel free to attach the cord to another socket to check if it still functions so that you can outline where the problem came from and fix it.

## Examine the HDMI cord/cable connections:

Make sure that you check the HDMI connection ports thoroughly. The cable connection might be loose, and if that is the case, then you will be getting lots of interruption with video signals. That is where the no signal message is with the

Stick. You can also try another cable to be sure that your cord functions perfectly because the problem can be from the cables.

## Examine how the HDMI port functions:

The problem can also come from the HDMI port hardware. Firstly, remove the cable from the HDMI port and reconnect it in fifteen seconds. It that did not solve the issue, then you should utilize another HDMI port.

## Choose the right resolution:

If you have an incorrect resolution, it

can hinder streaming with the Stick. So you should ensure that you select the right resolution that is compactable with the Stick. Do that by tapping the up and rewind control keys on the Stick remote, select use current resolution.

## Examine your cyberspace network:

Ensure that your cyberspace network is active with enough speed. If you have a slow network, it can affect your streams and make it very complicated.

## Firestick overheating

## Utilize HDMI Extender

The Stick has an HDMI extender inside its box. You can utilize the extender to connect the Stick to the television. Whenever you do not utilize the extender, the Stick stays very close to the television, and that can block the flow of air. The TV also produces heat, and that will not let the Stick cool off, and it can cause overheating for it.

# Low charge

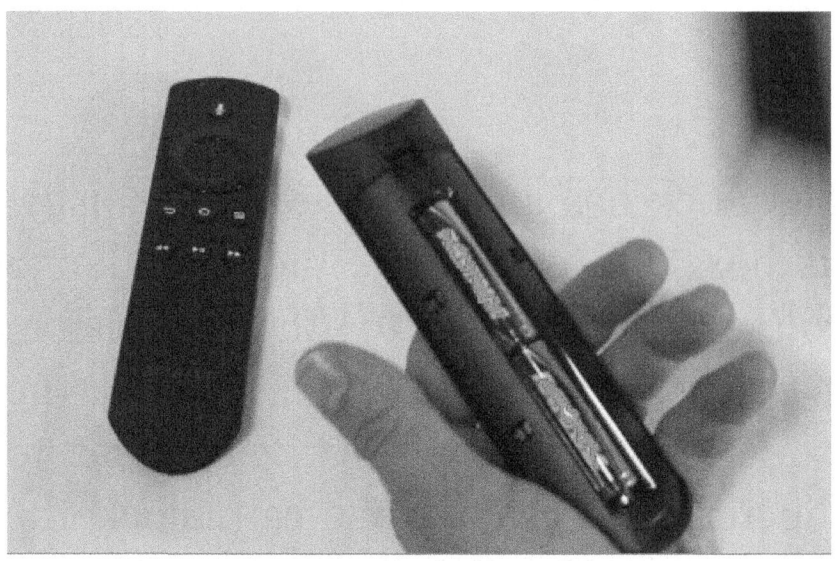

Check the connection to the HDMI port and connect it properly, and it should solve the problem. Ensure that the mechanism charges fully with the right cord.

## Issues with motherboard

If the Stick stops working because of those problems, it is time to purchase a new one.

## Not connecting with television

The best solution is reloading and repair. Turn the mechanism off and on and ensure that you charge the battery fully. Tap the home control key for about ten seconds to repair.

## Low batteries

Whenever your battery gets low, you should replace them immediately. Also, check that the battery contact with the metal.

## Issues with buttons

Whenever you start getting this type of problem, you should replace the remote buttons.

## Receiving gadget goes mute

You can solve this problem by simply increasing your volume.

# Issues with connecting external speakers

If you encounter this problem, you should switch the settings for audio to default.

## HDMI issues

Plug the machine to another gadget to check. If you still have that issue. Change the port.

## Insert the Stick inside the television side panel

Lots of television have two or more HDMI inputs. There are also inputs at the side and back of the television. The Stick can go to the back, but it will not get adequate air. However, if it goes to the side, it will be more exposed to air because it can get enough air on the side.

## Clear Cache for heavy apps

Anytime you launch an application on the Stick, it saves a cache on the gadget storage. The larger the application, the bigger the Cache. Just clear the Cache regularly.

Tap settings from the Stick home

Select apps

Tap control Installed apps

Choose the application and tap clear

cache.

Force-close applications to enable them to run in the background

Some applications continue to run in the background after exiting it. The application can get stuck or freeze, and you should tap the home key to return to the stick layout.

## Launch settings from the home visual display

Tap apps

Tap control obtained applications

Choose the application to exit

Tap force-close.

Unplug the Stick so that it can refresh

When you force close an application or clear your Cache, it helps the Stick avoid overheating problems.

## Eradicate applications you don't need

One major issue the stick face is the problem of storage spaces. The Stick has an 8gb storage space, but when you compare that to file sizes in this modern-day, that kind of storage space will fill up very fast. You should delete any application not needed to avoid overheating.

# Eradicate APK files after you install third-party applications

Before you sideload apps, firstly, get their APK files on the stick storage. After installing the application, you do not need the apk files anymore. But you should know that they did not leave the computer entirely, so you have to eradicate them yourself to avoid overheating.

## Reset the Stick

Reset the Stick if all the above steps do not solve the problem, resetting will take the gadget back to its factory settings. It removes the apps you have installed.

The steps below will guide you to reset your Stick.

Launch settings

Proceed to my TV

Tap Reset.

## The fire stick remote stops working

A lot of things can cause this problem starting from the Stick, TV, and the remote. Access them one after the other, and you will solve the issue, and the remote will resume function perfectly.

## Examine the remote stick batteries

After using the Stick for some time, you

would know about its regular battery issues, so if the remote stops working abruptly, the first thing you should check is the battery. It is empty, and you should replace it.

# Conclusion

This book contains several important information and methods of easily utilizing the Amazon fire stick. The concepts in this book give users a good understanding and excellent explanation of the Stick and how to use it. You will start with a general introduction to fire Stick, how to use it, and different tasks to perform with the device. The variation between fire television and its

Stick. How to set up and several tips for the fire stick. You will also get to understand the capabilities of the Stick, different applications that you can use with the Stick, and several tips for troubleshooting on the device.

Made in the USA
Monee, IL
13 December 2020

52751226R00083